ED & THE
SHELTER CATS

ALL PROCEEDS BENEFIT SHELTER ANIMALS

Illustrations by:
Andrea Weir
Weir Studios
Ocean Park, Washington

Edited by:
Rodney L. Merrill
Elite Word & Image
Astoria, Oregon

Published by:
Rivertide Publishing
www.rivertidepublishing.com

ISBN-978-0-9826252-5-5

Printed in South Korea

ED & THE SHELTER CATS

Ed Halula

FOREWORD

I had the pleasure of volunteering with Ed Halula at the local animal shelter. He was "one of those," a cat person, and I worked with the dogs. However, we both worked on the shelter Facebook page where Ed wrote cat stories and I wrote impressions of adoptable dogs. I also embellished shelter animal photos in hopes of making them more eye catching. And that's how our artistic partnership began.

While my dog write-ups were fairly prosaic, Ed's cat stories were fanciful and, well, eccentric. Embellishing ordinary photos to illustrate his stories raised my freak flag to full mast. Each time the photos rose to the task, Ed would create a more outlandish story to see how I would respond. Rarely have I laughed so much while doing the serious job of getting animals noticed and adopted.

We no longer work together and my photo illustrations are not legally mine to use here. But in a way that is for the best. Good fortune bestowed upon this project the fanciful illustrations of Andrea Weir. Her cats perfectly complement Ed's stories.

While Ed's stories and Andrea's artwork are pleasing in their own right, the icing on the cake is dedicating all of the hard work and the resulting proceeds to good health and good homes for shelter animals.

Rodney Merrill
Astoria, Oregon

"Name the different kinds of people," said Miss Lupescu. "Now."
Bod thought for a moment. "The living," he said. "Er. The dead."
He stopped. Then, "Cats?" he offered, uncertainly.

Neil Gaiman, The Graveyard Book

PREFACE

Volunteering at animal shelters for a combined three years, I chose to work exclusively with the cats. Knowing cats were generally viewed as second class citizens to dogs, my aim was to help level the playing field. It seems human nature to "root for the underdog," but still, this decision on my part surprised me. I had always considered myself strictly a dog person. In fact, I never had much of a fondness for cats. But, as you'll see, the cats won me over, won me over bigtime!

Among the myriad of tasks the shelter assigned to me were the cleaning of cat cages and working the adoption room, showing and telling potential adopters about the cats. To promote the adoption of particular cats, the volunteers were asked to write factual accounts describing their appearance, personality and behavior. I took this task a step further and told of the cats in creative and fanciful fashion. My write-ups appeared on the shelter's Facebook page, and I was utterly amazed when I started to receive positive reaction to my stories from around the country and as far off as England.

This led to me doing this book which includes a selection of that writing. I've also included other cat stories, some are fantasy while others tell of cats in my life outside the shelter. While volunteering I was constantly told by friends and acquaintances that they could never volunteer themselves. They'd feel too sorry for the animals. Well, I admit I shed a few tears, but happy tears far outnumbered the sad. And keep in mind, while far from ideal, shelters provide animals with a secure home when they need it most.

I thank two very talented friends who assisted with the book. Rodney Merrill served as the editor, and Andrea Weir served as the illustrator. Without their encouragement, creativity and hard work this book would not have been possible.

CAT TALES

Dedicated to the cats who stretched out their
little paws and touched my soul.

I will remember them forever.

There are cats waiting at the shelter right now who are every
bit as charming and beautiful as the ones I describe in these
stories. Visit your local shelter. You may find a lovable furry
friend who will deepen your life in ways you never imagined.

SAMANTHA

I told my adoption room partner, DeAnna, about it, but she just rolled her eyes. Yet, not five minutes later I saw the cat do it again. When I rushed to tell DeAnna, her response sounded as if she might be getting a little irritated.

"Ed, you mean to tell me that new cat can twitch her nose? Please Ed," she said, giving her head a little shake. "You've been watching too much TV, or maybe you're starting to believe that fantasy stuff you write."

I cooled it with DeAnna. She didn't want to hear anymore. I get it. I could hardly believe it myself. But I kept an eagle eye on Samantha, our coy new cat, and that nose. Perhaps no one else knows, but I know this cat's nose twitches. And when it does... good things happen! It's like Samantha casts a magical spell and we become bewitched.

This lovely girl no more than entered the adoption room before she was out and about, socializing. Other cats, people, they all were the same to her. She got up close and personal with a friendly greeting.

Except for the kittens. Samantha didn't seem too thrilled with the kittens. I thought maybe she had never encountered kittens before. But she's an older cat, so maybe she's had her share of kittens and has had enough of the little critters.

Samantha is a dainty thing, rather petite and sleek. She is a gray and black tabby. Her coat has a certain gleam which makes her a very attractive older lady. And that twitching nose. I couldn't help myself and said to DeAnna, "Maybe it's only around me it twitches. Maybe Samantha is one of them cougars. You know, an older female who likes younger guys. And when she looks at me that nose goes into high gear."

DeAnna laughed so hard I feared she might crack a rib or two. "Only one who's going to be twitching their nose at you, Ed, is Father Time!" my dear friend exclaimed.

Speaking of time, you should set aside some for yourself and get over to the shelter to meet this very attractive and personable cat. Whether or not her nose twitches, Samantha seems to have magical powers about her. Don't be surprised if you, too, become bewitched and find yourself carting home a carrier with a smiling Samantha inside. And if you do, who knows? I propose keeping a close eye on her nose!

CLYDE

Okay folks, Clyde is anything but a conventional kitty. So you won't be surprised that I spied Clyde driving a 1952 Chevy Woodie (you know, one of those old station wagons with real wood paneling on the sides) in my neighborhood the other day.

That's right, he was sputtering down Sunset Boulevard at The Cove in Seaside. And yup, he had an Al Merrick® surfboard tied on top of that Woodie. Clyde was about to ride a few waves and, if I know Clyde, he probably was hoping he'd get to dodge a few sharks while doing it.

Take in that visual image and you'll pretty much know what kind of cat this three-year-old is. He's a feisty adolescent male.

The guy's adventuresome, always ready for action. So much so, he might start a small skirmish with another cat simply for something to do.

Clyde's not the cat for just anyone. You couch potatoes best find yourself a lap cat, not a surfer cat like Clyde. But if you are into daring action and morning to night fun, then Clyde just might be the one for you. Oh, he's a handsome cat, too, strutting around the beach in his silver tabby garb with pronounced black stripes.

Think of those stripes as tattoos on a fit young bod and you'll get a sense of the rebel nature of Clyde. Yeah, he's an active kitty and an instigator. But you will have to admit, he's awfully pretty, too. And, as I said, this dude Clyde is no conventional kitty.

Thus, I present to you, our Pet of the Week, the pride of our cat room, one cool guy named Clyde. He rides the waves, all right. And if you're up for a life of unending fun, see that he rides them homeward with you.

LIZA JANE & BUBU

Liza Jane is the mother, and BuBu is her son. He's also her moon and stars, for there's no greater love than that which shines between a mother and a son. They're nearly carbon copies, except for their size. Both are gorgeous, long haired, and arrayed in lily white with apricot. Think of fluffy clouds, exceedingly polite. Twinkling eyes set in cotton candy suggest a sweetness and innocence lying gently within.

I'll forego fancy imagery, though, when expressing their appeal. I can best reveal these cats by how they make me feel.

They sweep me off my feet, stealing my heart while it beats to the meter of a love poem. My weary feet become cheery, as I dance and hum along.

Both mother and son show signs of affection, yet remain quite reserved. But keep in mind, what I offer is a snapshot in time. With a bit of encouragement and a showering of love, these new arrivals soon will likely bloom. Adopt both or just one. If you feel poetry, dance or song, you won't go wrong. Neither Liza Jane nor BuBu is your common everyday cat. I trust my description of them has convinced you of that.

MAPLE

My owner, who I always called Mama, tucked a four leaf clover under my collar. Said it would bring me good luck. Mama kissed me and held me close for the longest time. As tears streamed down her face, she handed me to Mr. Rose. Mama then disappeared from my sight. I didn't know it at the time; but then again, maybe I had an inkling I would never see dear Mama again.

I was a kitten of six months when I went to live with Mama. She said my tortie coat was every bit as lovely as her native New England countryside in mid-October. The fall foliage of the maple tree, Mama said, best described me. I was a sweet kitten, too. Sweet as maple syrup, is what Mama said. So she named me Maple. I thought it was an especially nice name. That was two years ago in people time.

The neighbor, Mr. Rose, placed me in my carrier and drove me to the shelter. As his pickup sputtered and bounced along, Mr. Rose kept mumbling my name followed by, "It's a darn right shame."

I cried during the trip. I sensed I faced a great unknown. I do not like unknowns. Upon our arrival at the shelter, Mr. Rose told of Mama no longer being able to properly care for me.

"It's a darn right shame," he muttered once again.

"Maple here was Mama's pride and joy, too. Never have I seen a more gentle, affectionate and well-behaved cat," Mr. Rose exclaimed. "That cat's a treasure, and she grew up to be just like her Mama."

Lonely, forlorn, heart broken, there are no words to express how I felt. I was not happy to be in this new place and I let it be known. I might have been a bit nasty, but can you blame me?

The people at the shelter said I'd adjust, that my fussing and grumbling eventually would subside. Like many of our cats, Maple had experienced a difficult separation, they opined.

So here I sit, serving my time. And indeed, I'm growing calmer each day. Pretty much all I think about now is being cuddled and kissed again. But no more goodbye kisses, please. I want "hello" kisses. I want to have a new person, a new home, and a new beginning.

Mama believed in good luck. But I know her reason for giving me that four leaf clover was about more than luck. It was to forever remind me of time spent with Mama and how she gave me a good start in life. It was to remind me that I was loved and that I am lovable.

Please adopt me. Give me a chance. You'll be getting one terrific cat. I owe that much to Mama and I'll owe that much to you.

LILABELLE

Captivating, bewitching, enchanting and enthralling all describe the charming Lilabelle. Sprite, fairy, pixie and elf, there's a bit of each here, for there's magic in this young lady.

Lilabelle is a sweet little thing and mellow beyond her years. And she has a tendency to simply vanish. Once I wanted to introduce her to potential adopters, but she was nowhere in sight. So I proceeded to describe Lilabelle to them, noting she was a rather petite, brown and white, ticked tabby. The visitors then asked what Lilabelle was upset about.

"No, no, no," I explained. "Ticked refers to the pattern of her coat, not to her state of mind."

When Lilabelle reappeared I introduced her in what I thought would be a clever fashion: "This is Lilabelle, an empty nester." Hearing that intro, Lilabelle vanished as if she had simply melted into the floor.

Lilabelle later explained to me that she thought I said, "Lilabelle, this is Sylvester."

After having two litters in her first year, she didn't want to meet any Sylvester, or Garfield, Rufus or Tom, for that matter.

"Had more than enough of THAT!" exclaimed the exhausted and wary Lilabelle.

VICTORIA

Forthwith, I report on my audience with the Queen. Trumpets sound as I enter the Great Hall. Just in time, too, to witness Queen Victoria plop her royal behindness onto the throne. Actually, the throne belonged to me, and was me, since my lap was the nearest.

Oh yes, Victoria loves sitting on laps and, in fact, upon nearly every lap in her Queendom she has sat. Our Queen is quite stunning in appearance. She's cast in the mold of her namesake, the renowned Victoria, moving about in close proximity to her castle's floor, while carrying a tiny bit of extra portage. The sparkling of our Queen's gray hair rivals the diamonds of any crown.

Victoria is most gracious, too, when she wants to be. She purred melodically for my ears and even allowed my commoner hands to stroke her silky gown, up, down, and all around. When I asked Her Majesty if my petting should cease, she frowned, hissed and took a swat.

Yes, our Queen shows a bit of royal impatience and attitude at times. The impertinence of other cats, in particular, ruffle her fur. Nevertheless, I stole me a kiss before being dismissed. If that little smooch qualifies me as Victoria's Prince, I'd find living with her most charming.

LITTLE BEE & LITTLE BEAR

LITTLE BEE

Should you adopt Little Bee, you'll be adopting her longtime friend as well. She came to us accompanied by a large brown teddy bear, who we dubbed Little Bear. We'd never dream of separating them.

Little Bee is a senior cat, petite in stature, black in color, and a reserved, quiet little soul. She stays at the back of her cage and could be easily overlooked if it wasn't for her bright yellow eyes peering out at you. Those mellow, yet penetrating, eyes captivated me. They drew me to Little Bee and I made a concerted effort to get to know her.

A sweet little lady she is. Little Bee is now affectionate with me, in her cautious, reserved way. She'll make a tremendously devoted companion to someone giving her a quiet home. I can assure you, get to know her and she will melt your heart.

LITTLE BEAR

If you're familiar with Ed's writing, you're accustomed to talking cats. They seem almost normal by now. But now it's a talking bear. What's more, a talking stuffed bear. That's right, I'm Little Bee's tawny talking teddy bear.

Bee and I have always been together and we intend to stay that way. As hard as it is for a stuffed bear to talk, I simply must speak up. We need to get Bee adopted, and soon. She's none too happy right now. Her owner recently died, leaving Bee after many loving years. Bee hasn't handled it well and it's sad to see her this sorrow stricken.

I used to see sunbeams radiating from Bee's eyes. Now I see only hurt. How do we explain to Bee that her lady is never coming back, that forever they'll be apart? Excuse me, Ed. Where's that box of tissues?

"A talking stuffed bear?" you ask. "A crying stuffed bear?"

As Ed says, "Whatever it takes to find Little Bee a home."

CHANCE

Kind of warm in here. They said this spacesuit was air conditioned, but maybe they forgot us cats can't remove our coats. Can't turn my head much either. Hard to look very far to either side wearing this fish-bowl-like helmet. Tired of looking only straight ahead. A fish bowl would be better.

Here I go again, thinking of FOOD! Yeah, a couple of nice, juicy fish would taste pretty good right now. A whole lot better than that freeze dried stuff we have on board. Package says "salmon," but it tastes more like cardboard.

When I agreed to do Cat Outreach, I had no idea of what I was getting myself into! "Outreach" all right, reaching all the way to the stars! So here I sit, onboard this cramped rocket ship headed to a planet called Durth.

Houston tells me we're six days from landing. Pretty boring just sitting here. Pretty, pretty boring. Once in awhile I fiddle with a dial or two, but the computers run most everything, just like back on Earth.

And that reminds me, you know that moon that circles the Earth? They say it looks like Swiss cheese. Well, that's exactly what it is! But that's not the half of it. That big old cheese ball is swarming with mice. And here I sit, nearly starving, eating salmon-flavored cardboard while there's all those delicious mice just beyond my window.

There I go again, thinking of FOOD! Oh, how I'd like to chomp down on a juicy mouse or two. Crunchy on the outside, soft on the inside. I can imagine tasting those luscious flavors.

(KA-BOOM!)

We've landed, folks. So here I am on planet Durth, about to meet my first Durthlings. I'm coming, I'm coming, for other-worlds-gods-sake, how fast do you think I can move in this spacesuit? And where'd they get the idea of calling this THING a spacesuit? You have about as much space in it as sardines in a can! Oh, there I go again, thinking of FOOD!

Wonder what Durthlings eat? Wonder if they eat at all? Oh, surely not, surely they don't eat cats! Do they?

"Okay, Chance, strip." They want me to strip? The first words I hear uttered by Durthlings, utter strangers, and it's the word strip? This place might be more like planet Earth than I imagined! Here comes a Durthling now, pen, clipboard and checklist in hand.

"This one's named Chance. He's shown as a Siamese mix. Love those blue eyes. His coat I'm recording as cream and taupe with a bullseye pattern. Quite a unique and handsome specimen we have here. His bio chip reads: Nearly blind, sees only faint images out of left eye and nothing out of right. Poor guy. Really friendly, though."

"Okay, Chance, stand over there. You're being adopted by the Durthlings."

Oh, really now, how many light years from Earth? And I'm finally getting adopted! Oh my, not so I can be eaten, I hope!

There Chance goes again, always thinking of FOOD!

ANGIE

It's her eyes. She has lovely melon green eyes which contrast stunningly with her dilute tortie coat. Seldom does anyone fail to comment on Angie's beauty when first meeting her. But it's not the color of her eyes that has taken hold of me, it's their direction!

If I'm in the adoption room, Angie's eyes are focused on me. Whether she is behind her cage door, or out in the room, Angie's eyes follow me. It's somewhat of a joke in the adoption room that Angie only likes males. I wouldn't say "only likes," but she sure has a preference for guys. Any guy walks into the adoption room, Angie's eyes fix upon him. Angie knows me well and her eyes reflect it. Frankly, I find it heart-wrenching. If Angie could fit into my own family, I'd take her home, but my other cats would never accept her.

Perhaps, she would fit into your family. She's an older cat; her elderly owner had to give her up due to health concerns. She'd be best in a quiet home with an older person.

Angie has been with us at the shelter a long while now. She had a difficult time adjusting to her life at the shelter; though, she's now settled in and her affectionate nature is shining forth. In fact, she's to the point now where more often than not she will follow my commands if there are no distractions in the room. She's one smart, older, sophisticated lady.

One recent afternoon Angie gave me my Valentine a few weeks early. I've never seen her do this before, but she turned over on her back, did a doggy paddle motion with her front legs and paws, while staring at me with her engaging green eyes. Break my heart, Angie, break my heart!

One day soon we are destined to part forever. Of one thing I am sure, a piece of my heart will go home with my dear Angie.

MICKEY

Glancing up, Mickey said, "Ed, give me another sheet." Ed, scuffling through a mound of crumpled paper, reluctantly handed Mickey another sheet.

"You know, Mickey," Ed said. "We've gone through an entire tablet and have nothing to show for it but crumpled paper."

Mickey, mildly protested. "But Ed, you wanted me to write about myself, and this writing business is none too easy." Mickey looked down with a frown and began to write. "Okay, I've got it. Here, read this."

Ed then read, "Hello, it's me. . .That's it? I know I told you to introduce yourself, but I meant for you to tell about yourself so people will want to adopt you. Tell them about you being a laid back, older, but loving cat. Tell them how you're extremely shy, but if a person takes the time to know you, they'll become very attached.

"You're much like velcro in that respect. There's much to be said, Mickey, about your steadfast loyalty once you accept someone. Take, for example, those two kittens. They head right over to you all the time now and the three of you cuddle. You're destined to be a loner no longer, Mickey, since you've opened yourself up to Scooter and Dash.

"It may sound corny, Mickey, but those amazing yellow eyes of yours remind me of maize. And your coat, why it's the color of a moonless night. You're a lean, slim guy, Mickey. You could stand to gain some weight. But wait, you were to write about yourself. You tricked me, and I took the bait!"

"Okay Ed," Mickey said. "I'm finished now, here's my post."

Ed then read what Mickey handed to him: "I'm everything Ed said, plus I'm an exceedingly handsome guy!"

Ed looked at Mickey, and then winked and gave an approving nod. "Yes, you're all of that, Mickey, but you forgot one thing. You're also a most lovable guy!"

DITTO

Behind the frosted window panes, you're warm and comfy at night. The fire blazes, you feel content, and all seems quite right. She moves slightly about, but she's still asleep in your lap. You marvel at your good fortune. You pat her head, and then stroke her chin. You smile, and then you grin.

"What an exquisite Christmas treat!" you tell yourself. For you gifted yourself that cuddly mass of marshmallows and licorice now awake and stirring in your lap. She peers up at you and begins to purr through half-closed eyes.

Ditto is now living with you and owning your heart, as she will from now on, day in and day out. The moment you saw her, she reminded you of marshmallows due to her soft and fluffy white fur. Her black fur was licorice to you, so shiny and sweet. Long-haired black and white cats are particularly gorgeous, and they usually end gloriously like Ditto, with a long swishing tail.

Her dazzling coat seems to mimic her manner. She's cuddly, soft, and gentle in her ways. Yet her marshmallow demeanor has a slight twist of licorice to it. She's very sweet, but occasionally a bit of edginess appears. You recognize it may be a learned trait in your cat of eight years, as Ditto previously lived with three other cats. There's always a bit of friction in a household like that.

Put yourself into this story. Give yourself Ditto this Christmas. You and Ditto write the subsequent chapters. "Marshmallows and Licorice," what a sweet, enticing title for an autobiography about you and the cat you'll forever love.

A HALLOWEEN OF LONG AGO

I've been writing about our cats for nearly three years. Promoting cat adoption, though, began sixty years ago. It was Halloween, 1957, and I was eight years old.

My grandmother had a cat named Rachael that marched to the beat of a different tom-tom. Never did she frolic with a tom in the spring or summer like most queens. Rachael did her romancing in the off season. She once presented a litter at Christmastime. A year or so later, Rachael delivered five kittens on Labor Day, giving an entirely new meaning to the holiday.

We lived in a rural village where cats were plentiful. No one showed much interest in adopting the Labor Day litter, and by late October, Grandmother became concerned. Then my younger brother, along with three other playmates and I, took the matter into our own hands.

Kids back then commonly wore long underwear during the winter. After a bit of trading among ourselves, we produced five pairs of long underwear in various colors. I dismantled an old broom. It's bristles became our whiskers. Mother's snagged nylon stockings were stuffed with newspapers. We had our tails. With a pair of tin snips and a few empty tin cans, pointed ears were created. We entered the village Halloween Parade as a clowder of determined alley cats.

Carrying placards advertising Rachael's kittens for adoption, we took home first prize in the parade. And within a few days, the townsfolk took home all but one of Rachael's kittens.

The remaining kitten was the runt of the litter. He was frail, lame, and unruly, and one eye was partly closed. His coat was best described as dirty white with a pallid orange spot encircling his rear.

For the first time in my young life, I witnessed how cruel mankind can be. That poor kitten was ridiculed by those who came to see him. He was called "ugly" and "evil looking." One man even suggested we drown him.

While looking after the little guy, that orange spot on his rear gave my brother and me an idea for a name. Grandma approved calling him "Pumpkin," but "Butt" for his last name? Grandma told us we should be ashamed!

My parents had never allowed a family pet. But because they were so impressed by our initiative in getting Rachael's kittens adopted, they agreed to let us keep Pumpkin. In retrospect, I suspect they agreed, thinking he wouldn't live long.

While Pumpkin never qualified as a show cat, he lived more than fifteen years. Grandma always said Pumpkin knew we loved him far too much for him to die on us.

Today, Pumpkin and Rachael lie next to each other on a certain hillside in western Pennsylvania. Last summer, I visited them for the first time in forty years.

Standing there, I relived memories of the two cats, fingering recollections like beads on a rosary. Only then, through the distance of those many years, did I come to fully appreciate how those two innocent creatures had invested the most utterly ordinary place with magic, and how they helped to shape the person I am today. I am so grateful for them.

The shelter has a roomful of Pumpkins and Rachaels patiently waiting to enrich your family's life in ways unimagined, but real nonetheless. Waiting to conjure up memories with your family that will never die. They are waiting for you. All you have to do is say, "Yes."

CLAIRE

It was late Spring, 2002. The pervasive shivering caused by the chill of the night had long abated. Long gone were the hunger pains. A numbness, both physical and mental, had taken hold. Claire was no longer aware of her kittens. The ditch serving as their home was rapidly filling with rainwater. The mother and her litter awaited their release from this world. Their cruel and unfair suffering would soon be over.

As a final earthly gesture, Claire cried out. It was a death cry, but you might easily imagine it was a plaintiff, yet profound question, "Why?" A mental image of her own mother coming to take her may have prompted Claire's cry.

A few short weeks later, the shelter staff had nursed Claire back to health. The Good Samaritan who rescued her and her kittens visited weekly. Then one day, he found Claire was gone. Yes, she had been adopted. It was not surprising. Claire was a gorgeous young cat, a chocolate point Siamese with sparkling sapphire eyes. And she projected a serene and sweet manner.

Claire spent the next fifteen years in a most loving and caring home. However, much like Claire's life before being adopted, her new family was beset with ongoing tragedy. It was a family broken twice by divorce and twice by the death of siblings. Unable to find housing that would accept a pet, the mother and the remaining child had to give up yet another longtime family member, their beloved Claire.

Claire has traveled a long journey. She was in Georgia when she was born and rescued from the ditch. She's now a senior in need of a new home. Claire's cream coat has darkened over the years. She is still a beautiful cat. And she's a sweet cat, a tremendously sweet cat.

I interviewed her previous owner for this story. As did the person who rescued Claire long ago, the relinquishing owner and her remaining daughter visit Claire frequently. I was moved as she told Claire's history with the cat resting contently in her lap. When the woman finished her tale and stood up to leave, the cat cried out. It was a haunting shrill siren dirge that transported me to Claire crying out from that ditch long ago.

Claire is crying out once again for someone to help. Perhaps you're the someone who will mend this sweet girl's twice broken heart. And please, God, if you would ensure that it is the last dear Claire must endure.

JAX

As a child you may have played the game of Jacks. Bouncing a rubber ball in the air and gathering up metal jacks spread across the table. You only had a brief period to accomplish your task before the ball bounced a second time.

Interacting with our five-year-old cat, named Jax, is like playing Jacks. He loves his head petted and his chin rubbed, but only for a brief period. Then the ball bounces a second time and your opportunity passes. We make the most with those openings with Jax, giving him as much attention as we can before Jax withdraws again. Jax has made real progress; but it's been slow in coming.

Jax came to the shelter as a stray who was quite battered. We nursed his physical wounds, restoring his appearance. But it was obvious Jax had emotional wounds that needed healing, too. Through a great deal of patience, time and love from the volunteers, Jax has been recovering emotionally as well as physically. The rubber ball still bounces a second time for him and the moment passes, but the span of time for gathering together is growing longer by the day.

We can only do so much at the shelter. What Jax needs most to bring about his complete recovery is stability and consistency; a secure, loving home. This is where you enter the game. You could make all the difference in Jax's life and, at the same time, make all the difference in your own life.

We all have Jacks waiting to be gathered and good deeds waiting to be done. Adopting Jax and giving him a new start is now on your table. Ensure you'll be a winner in the game of life. Score while you still have time. For, like all of us, one day your rubber ball will bounce a second time.

A DREADFUL CHRISTMAS EVE

'Twas the night before Christmas, everyone was in bed.
The house smelled of clove and sweet gingerbread.

Not a creature was stirring, not even a soul.
The house mouse was snuggled, asleep in his hole.

The stockings, they hung on the chimney with care.
The tree was all tinseled with extravagant flair.

That is, 'til the family cat took on a dare,
and swiped a red stocking to add to his lair.

Santa's milk and his cookies were next to be seized,
replaced by the cat with pieces of cheese.

Aroused by the smell, the tiny house mouse,
sprang from his bed, and sped through the house.

Crossing the living room in record time,
he dined on the cheeses, so pleasing and fine.

When the house mouse was down to the very last bite,
out from the chimney came a frightening sight.

The cat like a flash did suddenly appear,
grinning and toothy from ear to ear.

The cat didn't think his plan might be a bust.
Certain the mouse would be his for breakfast.

He'd conquer the mouse, all fair and square,
shaking and baking it back in his lair.

He lunged at the mouse, but he was shutout.
His stocking was empty, his meal was in doubt.

A skirmish ensued, all through the house,
but the cat never caught up to that tasty mouse.

The cat lost the mouse and ate kibble instead.
The house mouse, belly bulging, retired to his bed.

Mouse was not sleeping, he was insomnolent.
Turns out the guy was lactose intolerant.

Rolled up in a ball and clutching his knees,
house mouse was groaning and *cutting the cheese.*

And stuck in the chimney, it's hard to believe,
was comatose Santa with barf on his sleeve!

Some say that Santa succumbed to the fumes
that seemed to be permeating all of the rooms.

This fright before Christmas was dreadful that eve,
and may be a story you might not believe.

When telling this tale at some future date,
please do be careful who you implicate.

Don't blame the cat, because don't you see,
it was entirely the fault of the cheese.

STELLA

One Saturday I attended an orientation for new volunteers. While standing alone in the lobby, I heard a faint whispering.

"Hey, fella!" That was followed by an equally faint, "Pssst, over here!"

I glanced to my right and spotted a tuxedo cat intently focused on me.

"Yep, that was me summoning you, fella," said Stella. "A lot of people think cats don't talk. But we certainly do. I suspect you already know that, though, don't you, Ed?"

I moved closer to Stella's cage, for what I was hearing was but a whisper.

"Ed, you looked uncomfortable standing over there not knowing anyone. I understand how you were feeling, though. Much like I did," Stella conjectured. "I'm new here, myself, Ed. Been at the shelter only a few weeks. But hey, people around here are friendly; so relax, Ed. They'll welcome you as they did me. In fact, they received me with open arms after my owner died.

"I'd been living in a quiet and caring home for all of my nine and a half years, since I was just a kitten. Now I find myself at the shelter just waiting. Waiting for another loving human and the security of a new home."

"You appear to be a wonderful cat," I replied. "Love your coat. To me, you're visual poetry, wrapped in midnight and highlighted with white starlight, ever so bright. Obviously, you can be social and outgoing, too, considering how you reached out to me. I hear that you don't like dogs, Stella. But rest assured, there are plenty of quiet, loving homes out there without a dog. Plenty of cat-people, as well, who will appreciate the serenity and comforting nature of a mature and fabulous feline like you."

Now, I'm here to speak up for Stella. She's a tested and worthy companion, offering an abundance of unconditional love. Might you be that special someone to reach out to her? If you do adopt her, be prepared to give Stella your undivided attention, because she will be intent upon making a cat whisperer of you, too.

CLANCY

Clancy is a dandy. I mean that in both meanings of the word. In fact, the term seems tailor-made to describe this young male cat. His appearance reminds me of a dandy; a fancy young man or a fop, if you will. It doesn't stretch the imagination much to visualize this young cat in a top hat, white silk gloves and tails, wearing a gold watch fob and twirling a gentleman's walking cane. It's the fastidiousness portrayed by this image which, to me, depicts Clancy.

His absolutely gorgeous dark brown tabby coat is so very crisp and clean, while appearing velvety with a sheen. The coat is highlighted with glistening jet black stripes accented by the classic bullseye pattern. He is simply stunning.

Clancy's personality is dandy, too. But not that of an affected, fancy young man. Nothing pretentious or contrived. Clancy's personality is dandy in the other meaning of the word, being extremely fine. He's friendly, exceptionally outgoing, and acts as if you're his best buddy when first meeting you.

When Clancy entered the adoption room, we were blown away. We couldn't believe what a charming, delightful young cat he was. Yes, a dandy. The term is tailor-made.

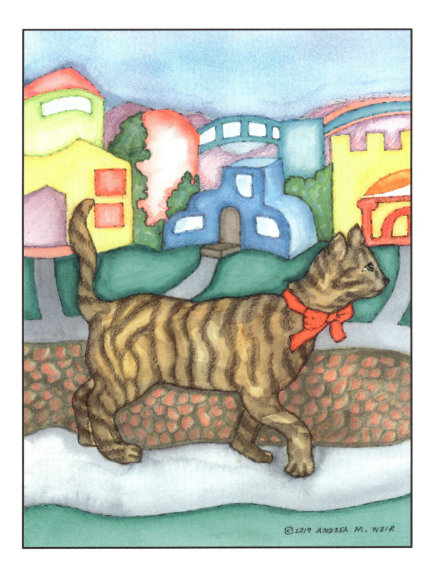

CLEMENTINE

They march, they drum, they toot and they twirl. The cats are on parade. Batons spin through the air, hopefully to be caught, but often they are not. Marching feline feet aligned perfectly to the beat of the drums in the street.

The cats step high to a steady beat through the oppressive heat. Fans come from far and wide, even from the countryside, to witness the cats on parade.

First up are the marching orange tabbies, sporting blazing flames on the end of their batons. Brilliant hues of gold and orange fire bleed from the street. This spectacular show of color is accompanied by the thunderous sound of percussion and brass, as the tabby drum and bugle corps marches alongside the flame-twirling tabbies. Eyes wide and paws over ears, the crowd watches as the tabby procession parades down the street and fades to glowing embers.

Next are the tuxedo cats, all black and white, and a delightful sight. This contingent has its own larger-than-life color guard of a zebra, penguin, panda and skunk, likewise costumed in the traditional black and white. The tuxedo cats pause to dance because there's a fiddle playing Hey Diddle Diddle, and then the black and whites parade by.

Up next are the tortoiseshell cats, and spectators see a gigantic turtle moving into view. It's an impressive tortie float, too. The turtle's name, Bertie, is painted on his shell. Bertie's not too sturdy; he bobs from side to side. Bertie's head seems to float as it turns and his eyes slowly open and close as if Bertie is getting flirty with one and all. The exuberant crowd cheers wildly as the tortie cats pass by.

By far the most colorful unit in the entire parade now comes marching by. It's the calico cats. A glorious rainbow of orange, white, and black stretches as far as the eye can see. This all-female legion receives a wild reception. The crowd erupts in cat calls and exclamations of "cat dolls!" The calico cats strut on.

Next comes the Queen's Float, a castle encircled by a moat. It dreamily floats by while spectators wave and rave and cry. Clementine, our queen, is a stunning Maine Coon wearing the traditional long coat which sports a dazzling array of browns, tans and grays, with white bib and stockings.

Rumors abound that our queen is people-oriented and an excellent lap cat. But she despises competition from vassals and desires to be the only cat in the castle.

So there you have it, folks. Orange tabbies, tuxedos, the torties and the calicos have all paraded by. Followed by our reigning queen, the lovely Miss Clementine, considered far and wide to be the fairest maiden of our time.

DOMINO

I envision Domino walking into the shelter on his hind legs, wearing tattered jeans and a badly torn and soiled t-shirt, his few earthly possessions carried in a 'bindle dangling from the end of a broomstick and slung across his shoulder.

Hobo Domino might be the characterization of this cat upon arrival. His tuxedo coat covered with fleas, his long lean frame malnourished, his demeanor a portrait of terror. Yes, he had been a stray. More than likely for many a day.

The fleas were the easy part, though they required a double treatment. We allowed him all he would eat. For days, several weeks in fact, he hid at the back of his cage. We caught only glimpses of his distinctive, triangular mask.

Through patience and persistence the cat volunteers won this guy over. Domino won the volunteers over as well. Won over each heart, toppling each and every one, like a spill of dominoes.

For all he had been through, this guy proved to be the most affectionate, most engaging, most lovable of cats. Domino is wildly popular among the volunteers; in fact, he's now the heartthrob of the adoption room.

From Hobo to Heartthrob, that's our Domino. Just in time for Valentine's Day, too. Come meet your true love. Come meet the inimitable Domino.

ASH & ZEB

Ash wants to say a little something about Zeb.

I first met Zeb the day I was born. I don't remember that day, of course, but he was there. Our mother died that day, too, so perhaps it's best I don't remember.

I never knew my mother. All I've ever known of family is Zeb. He tells me we were raised in a foster home. Zeb's a year older than me and has been with me every day of my three and one half years. Zeb was always there to comfort me, to play with me, to help me learn.

He was always the strong one, the quiet one, the courageous one. But he was also always the shy one. I never realized this about Zeb until I grew older. I then recognized that I was the more outgoing one. I noticed my big brother had started deferring to me. I became the protector, the one who stood out, the one fussed over.

I always knew the strong, quiet, courageous Zeb was there to support me. This allowed my personality to flourish. You might say, in this respect, I overshadowed Zeb. But I always knew Zeb was my rock and my foundation. Zeb was not only my older brother, but in a sense, my substitute mother.

I love Zeb. He's really all I ever had. It's been said that I'm the more attractive one, with my silky, silver gray coat and sparkling eyes. I always doubted this myself. Beauty is in the eye of the beholder. Zeb seems plenty attractive to me. His brown and black tabby coat is warm, soft and cuddly. I can attest to that. And, besides, mustering up courage you don't come by naturally to protect those you love is pretty attractive.

Our person recently had to give us up. Here at the shelter we're up for adoption. Up for adoption separately, so I don't know that Zeb will always be a part of my life. Nice if we were adopted together, but we can't be sure of that.

What I can be sure of is that Zeb will always be in my heart. No matter what the future brings, I know the two of us will make the most of it. Our new person (or people, if we end up apart) will be proud of us. We'll make the mother I never knew proud of us.

Most of all, Zeb, we'll live a life which will make us proud to call each other brother.

Love you bro, your Ash.

A LITTER BEFORE CHRISTMAS

It occurred in the mid-1950s. I'm not certain of the exact year, but it now seems a lifetime ago. I remember that period by three distinct events.

My grandfather bought a two-tone Buick, bright coral and white. It was the flashiest car in town back then. It would be a to-die-for car today. I watched Elvis Presley on the Ed Sullivan Show. For months thereafter, I went around wiggling my little behind while crooning. But most of all, I remember grandma's cat, Rachael.

One year, about a week before Christmas, Rachael gave birth to kittens. To this day I recall my grandmother's outrage and disbelief. "Cat's don't have kittens in winter!" my grandmother protested.

Apparently, Rachael didn't know that. Five little ones just in time for Christmas. My brother and I were thrilled, telling grandma it was Rachael's Christmas present to her.

"Huh!" replied grandma. And then she chased the two of us out the back door. Running around to the front door, we headed back to grandma's kitchen, pleading to be allowed to name the kittens. We decided on Christmas names: Rudolf, Santa, Snowflake and Angel. I insisted, though, the runt of the litter be called Baby Jesus.

Grandma wouldn't allow that name. She said we'd call him Jingles instead. My brother and I thought Jingles was a dumb name for a cat, so we called him Baby Jesus anyway.

Sometime later we learned from the neighbor, who gave Baby Jesus a home, that he was a she.

PATCH

Dear Lady Patch, allow me to introduce myself. I'm Abracadabra, the Magical Cat. I understand you're a shy and lonely girl. They say you're one of the most withdrawn cats they've seen at the shelter. So I've come to perform my magic.

First of all, my senior lady, I'll wrap you in this warm woolen blanket. Next, my stunning black on white lady, to protect your lovely head, I offer this cashmere scarf. And to cover your precious paws, try on these furry mittens.

Madame, if you'll allow me, I'll assist you onto my sleigh. Together we'll take a magical sleigh ride on this invigorating winter's day. So giddy-up horses, and away we go.

We're taking Patch on a sleigh ride through the snow, hoping to free her spirits and rejuvenate her soul. As the prancing horses lead the way, Abracadabra has much to say.

Look around you, Lady Patch, it's a magical world! Take, for instance, the glistening glow of the newly fallen snow. There's magic there, Lady Patch, in the way the snow mirrors your coat, so pristine and white. And look at old Mr. Crow over yonder pecking for food. There's magic in him, too. His coat resembles your patches, black as coal and shiny and bright.

Hello, Mr. Snowman! He says his name is Frosty, just like the air. Don't stare, Lady Patch, but he's a portly chap, round, or should I say slightly rotund? There's magic in him, too. It's his size, Lady Patch. The two of you are a good match when it comes to that.

Breathe deeply, Lady Patch, and take in the magic of this nippy air. Look at the bonfire over here. It's gleaming magic, warm and inviting. Just like your heart, Lady Patch. If only you'd let others see.

High in the sky I see Mr. Sun revealing himself from behind the clouds, greeting all with the magic of his warm embrace. Just as you'll do, Lady Patch, when you open yourself more fully to the human race. Slow down horse, into a steady trot. For I have a confession to make, Lady Patch.

Madame, I'm not a magical cat at all. I simply help others see the magic all about them, including the magic we all have within. I trust I've been able to reveal that to you, Lady Patch.

And I trust I've shown that to our readers. Let's hope the right one steps forward and adopts you, Lady Patch. Remember, dear readers, you each have the magic within to turn this timid cat into an accepting and affectionate companion. But you must have patience and believe. Abracadabra, believe in you! That's the real magic. I guarantee it's true.

BLACK CATS

As I write this, we have three black cats available for adoption. Two young ladies, Catherine and Paloma, both of whom seem to be constantly moving about impatiently and searching. Searching, even though they don't fully realize it, for a forever home and a family to call their own.

We also have a slightly older black cat, Miss Mouse, who is searching. But, until Miss Mouse goes to a permanent loving home, she seems content to search for someone who will pet her and reassure her that she's not alone.

I recently witnessed a potential adopter pass by these three cats. In each instance, the viewer muttered, "It's just a black cat." But no, these are not just black cats! They are much more than that. They are the color of the raven. And like the raven, they are silky, shiny and sleek. And like the raven, they have wings, though these wings, strong but unseen, are for lifting spirits.

They are not just black cats. They are the color of the night. And like the night, they offer you peace, serenity and the promise of a new day filled with hope, love and joy.

They are not just black cats. They are the color of anthracite, fueling you with the desire to love and to be loved back. And much like anthracite, they turn with time into diamonds, adding sparkle to your life. Like diamonds, or even diamonds in the rough, they will be treasured by you, day after day.

So no, Miss Mouse, Paloma and Catherine are not just black cats. In fact, they are everything that epitomizes cats: love, hope, companionship, security, caring.

Adopt any of these three ebony beauties and you can't go wrong. Each one is fabulous. You can then decide whether your cat is of the raven, the night, or anthracite. Each has poetry of her own.

A DAY AT THE ZOO

The cat-mobile arrives at the zoo. The cats exit in pairs and walk through the gate. BFFs Patti and Sally approach the admission booth and are told, "Sorry ladies, our free senior admission applies to those 55 and up."

"We're seniors," argues Patti. The admission clerk raises her eyebrows. Patti insists, "We're both ten years old, and we're CATS!"

"Thelma," says the admission clerk. "We have a couple of LIVE ones who don't want to pay."

"What's she saying, Patti?" Sally asks. "Dead people get in for free? If so, I'm out of here. You're not seein' no Sally walking around no zoo with no dead people! I won't even go near a cemetery, and dead people don't walk around there, at least not during the day."

"Calm down, Sally!" cries Patti. "Here comes that Thelma lady."

"Okay," says Thelma lady. "We don't want to argue with you. You may enter for free."

"Huh," Patti responds. "Hard enough for a lady to admit how old she is and then have to argue about being that old. Really! I get the feeling this place is a zoo."

"Patti," says Sally. "Let's sit on this bench and rest a while."

"Okay," Patti meows. "I've never been to a zoo before."

"Me either," Sally purrs. Then sliding into a bit of a yowl, she adds, "That former husband of mine would never go. Every time I asked him to take me to the zoo, I'd get the same response. He'd say, honey, if people want to see you, they can come to the house and look at you for free!"

"Who's this guy heading towards us?" Patti murmurs. "All smiles, he is. Hold on to your purse, Sally!"

"Good afternoon, ladies," oozes the smooth-talking man through his smile.

"What YOU want?" Patti yowls.

"I'm a zoo employee," says the still-smiling man. "I'm out today surveying visitors. May I ask you young ladies a few questions?"

"WE'RE NOT YOUNG!" Sally cries. "We've already been through that at the admission booth. And we're not giving you money to walk around your zoo, particularly when there might be dead people here who got in for free!" The zoo man's smile begins to wither.

"What kinda question you wanna ask?" Patti purrs.

"About the two of you is all," the man replies pleasantly. "I'd like to learn a little about the folks who come to the zoo."

"You go first, Sally," Patti says, sounding a little skeptical.

The man's smile returns. "Okay, ma'am, how old are you?"

"Oh, here we go again!" Sally mewls. "I'm a senior cat and leave it at that!"

"Okay, I understand," the man says tentatively. "What type of cat are you?"

"I'm a nice cat, that's the type I am. No matter what that former husband of mine might say. I'm pleasant, mellow and sweet, and I mind my own business, unlike you, sonny."

"No, ma'am," the man replies. "I meant what breed of cat are you?"

"You mean what I look like? I look GOOD!" Sally sputters. "Surely, you can see for yourself that..."

"Could you be more precise, ma'am?"

"Well, I'm a tortie, that's short for tortoiseshell. And don't you make slow turtle jokes either."

"No, ma'am," says the man, who now is less committed to his smile.

"We've wasted enough time," Sally grumbles. "Best look at some animals now. Let's visit the pumas. Least we can do, them being our relatives and all."

As Patti and Sally approach the puma cage, Sally exclaims, "Whoa! These pumas sure do STINK!"

"That reminds me," says Patti. "I need to use the ladies' room, and soon."

"Okay," Sally groans, as she slides back into a sitting position. "I'll stay here and visit with the pumas."

Patti mutters to herself, "Pumas, pumas, she wants to visit her stinky pumas while I go to the ladies' room. Fine. But I better get there quick before I PU-MA pants!" Then she chortles at her witticism.

BOO BOO BEAR

In the interest of full disclosure, I'll admit upfront this is one of my all time favorite cats. However, it took an experienced cat person, perhaps even a cat whisperer, to fully appreciate this guy. It's as though he was a stealth cat, hiding an exceptionally endearing personality under a defensive armor.

Bear and I connected early on, through the eyes. I was persistent in making eye contact with him. After a while, he realized I saw through his aloof facade. Several other volunteers, as well, were getting through to Bear.

For us, he became a total love bug. Hold Bear, cuddle Bear, squeeze Bear, talk sweetness and kindness to Bear, and he'd soak it up like a dry sponge. But let a member of the public or a volunteer he hadn't accepted enter the room and he instantly withdrew and hid away. This behavior was more dramatic and stark than I had ever seen in a cat, and it continued the entire time Bear was with us.

When the public caught glances of Bear, they invariably became interested. He was a handsome guy, his long, lanky body covered in a shiny, jet black coat. He moved with grace and agility, reminding you more of a panther than a domestic cat. Yet, I knew it would be difficult to get Bear adopted.

I wanted very badly to take him myself, but I already had four cats. I knew my home wasn't the best placement for Bear.

Eventually, Bear did find a home. Well, a third home. After being adopted twice and returned both times, the third time proved the charm. That day, when dear Bear finally found his permanent home, I was working the adoption room. I carefully placed him in a carrier, gave him a few gentle strokes, and bid him a cheerful goodbye.

Then I hid in the restroom and cried.

PEGGY

I've been here so long they now consider me family. "They," meaning the volunteers and particularly that wise guy, Ed. And about him; here's somethin' you should know. He ain't that wise; he just has a bit of wit and a sharp tongue. Nevertheless, I guess maybe he don't write half bad. Not half bad for him havin' only a third grade education.

Spilled the beans all over his dirty jeans, so to speak, didn't I? Serves him right, though, after him dubbin' me Little Ole Auntie Peggy. Says the name fits me purrfectly. Huh! Claims I remind him of an elderly spinster auntie nobody wants.

Huh, again! First of all, wise guy and third grade scholar, I'm not old. Since when is six years elderly for a cat? And I'm no spinster either! I'll have you know, cats don't marry. So how can I be beyond a marryin' age, if we don't marry?

Maybe CATS 101 was a fourth grade subject, and obviously you never got that far! And what do you mean by nobody wants me? Plenty of people would want me, if they only knew me.

If they don't know me, that's your fault, Ed. You're job is to write about me, tellin' the public how nice and pretty I am. But half of that fancy stuff you write, nobody reads. Nobody reads it, Ed! And in the other half they do read, there you are callin' me Little Ole Auntie Peggy with an uppity attitude.

No wonder I don't get adopted. Adding insult to injury, you write that my appearance reminds you of an old maid. Making smart remarks about my conservative gray dress with white shoes and a white, silky ascot. That's just the sort of thing that keeps folks away.

You write nothin' about how I love to lap sit and be petted. Not a word. Tell them people out there that I dare one of them to walk into the cat room and NOT find me landing in their lap and soakin' up their petting.

Oh sure, after awhile I may lose patience and fire off a little warning hiss or growl. But I'm harmless; just handle me as I request. And don't pick me up. On that I insist. Maybe Ed calls that uppity, but I call that a young lady's prerogative.

And so, Ed, my public awaits, in spite of what you do or don't write. Indeed, some lucky person will adopt me and, sometime soon, I predict. So there. Ole Auntie Peggy writes, setting the record straight. Make no mistake, little Eddie, your auntie can write every bit as well as you.

DUCHESS & CONTESSA

As the clattering of hooves comes to a stop, a carriage door swings open. Two charming young ladies exit and are escorted to the debutante ball. The Duchess wears a flowing black silk gown. Her stockings and feathery cravat are a shimmering white, as is the stick mask she holds up to cover her face. The Duchess' gorgeous bushy tail swishes, this way and that, as she regally steps onto the ballroom floor.

Lady Contessa is dressed in a smart, form-fitting gown. Rather than silk, it feels like suede. It, too, is black, but has a delicate repeating pattern in a color near caramel. The color also pervades her mask. Contessa's curiously curling tail sways, forward and back, as she ostentatiously steps onto the ballroom floor.

As the ladies' dance cards are being signed, their sweet and playful manner is noted by the toms. Their golden eyes glancing about reveal their inquisitive nature. The young ladies are elated, knowing new homes lie before them. The toms bow. The royal ladies curtsy.

As music fills the air, each tom whispers seductively: "Be my Ginger Rogers, for I'm your Fred Astaire."

CASEY

The outlook wasn't brilliant for the Mudville nine that day. Bottom of the ninth, two out, and it's "Casey at the bat." Casey rounds first and heads for second. In fact, he touches all the bases.

This is an exceedingly handsome cat, wearing pinstripes of dilute ginger trimmed in cream. Indeed, his uniform complements his genteel demeanor. Casey makes the All Star Team by virtue of his affectionate nature and his tendency to be demonstrative.

Pet this guy and he experiences rapture. He'll turn over onto his back, squiggle and squirm, and let go with a chorus of thunderous purrs. To further express his exuberance, I've seen Casey stretch out and roll back and forth, much like a rolling pin. This fellow epitomizes the joy found in owning a cat.

Casey hits it out of the park. The crowd roars as they watch him touch all the bases and head for home. Will Casey's home base be at your place? It likely will, if you're keeping score. This cat is a winner, and is sure to make a winner of Team You, too.

ORABELLE

With Orabelle you get two cats in one. No, she doesn't have a split personality. The duality arises in the contradiction between the visual image she projects and the manner in which she conducts herself.

Based upon her looks alone, you can envision Orabelle lounging in her boudoir, cloaked in a fine negligee, nibbling bonbons and puffing on a quellazaire, while effortlessly blowing a trail of well-formed smoke rings high into the air.

The terms "diva" and "prima donna" easily come to mind. She strikes the image of a haughty and sophisticated female feline. A cultured lady of great taste and grace, for beauty lies both within this cat and without. Orabelle has a silky long-haired coat. She's rather dainty, making an alluring sight dressed in her ashen gray and white.

The contradiction comes with Orabelle's behavior. You might suspect she's been cast in "West Side Story," and certainly she could be. She acts the part of a young female ruffian in a neighborhood of the Upper West Side. At times she's a bit nasty, as if she's streetwise and feels forced to preemptively protect herself. She freely chases after any cat within her sight.

With time and attention, this three-year-old should mellow. She doesn't like competition, though, so other pets and children must be kept away. She'd do best in a quiet home where she can rule the roost or, I should say, have the roost to herself. Always keep in mind, there's more than a diva and prima donna in the lovely Miss Orabelle.

MURPHY

Knock knock, who's there? Adore. Adore who? Adore is between us, open up. What, you ask, does a knock-knock joke have to do with Murphy?

Lamb Chop! I look at Murphy and think of the sock puppet made famous by Shari Lewis. Lamb Chop was known for knock-knock jokes. And if you knock, you'll find Murphy behind this particular door.

He's a rather large two-year-old boy who reminds me of a lamb. Look at that beautiful wool-like coat. It's warm, soft and cuddly. It's dense and luxurious, too. Rub your hands over a lamb's wool coat and you're petting our Murphy.

Color wise, too, Murphy sort of looks like dirty lamb's wool. A dusty covering in various shades of gray gives Murphy a unique, yet appealing appearance. Blue Point Siamese is certainly in Murphy's mix, and a lot of it, too.

Personality wise, there's also a bit of Lamb Chop in Murphy. Inquisitive by nature, this cat is playful and gets into all sorts of laughable situations. At times, he can be a bit feisty and obstinate, but I always find him lovable.

He's such a cute cuddly wuddly, you're always quick to forgive his antics. Like Lamb Chop, he's so sweet and vulnerable that your initial reaction is to pick him up and simply squeeze, squeeze, squeeze. You're so pleased, pleased, pleased with this most adorable character.

Better get your hand under this guy while he's still available. You'll have a playmate and best friend for life, and a love affair which will never end. I assure you, my friend!

ACHOO

Achoo, gesundheit! God bless you, Achoo. I must confess, when I first saw Achoo, I knew not what to do. No other cat looked like this Manx cat named Achoo. Seeing a cat like Achoo was for me something new. For here was a cat, kind of round and cuddly, with a tail that was stubby.

As I stared at Achoo and got a better view, I saw medium long hair that was silky and lush. Achoo's wrapping, and I swear this to you, gives him a cloak in the image of smoke. Many colors swirled together as if rising from a fire, shades of brown and gray and black as atop a smoke stack. A gorgeous sight.

A friendly young guy, I would say is true of Achoo. Loving and mellow is this handsome young fellow, too. What's more, he moves about with a slight hop. Although he has a rabbit-gait, he still can ambulate with the best of them.

This makes me want to shout and tell you all about this unique cat named Achoo and all he can do. Here's what you can do, if you, too, like Achoo. Come on down and sign the book, have a good long look, and soon you will be hooked.

Give this guy the loving home he never knew. God created this lovely creature, and may have created him just for you!

INDIAN SUMMER

The last of the mouse traps had been returned to the storage wigwam, the hunting party having been a huge success. The Cat-sop Indians now had enough mice and Uncle Ben's Rice to suffice for the winter. All regard this situation as quite nice.

While the tired braves from the hunting party unwind in the community wigwam, a drone delivery of fresh catnip arrives. As night approaches, the tribe's peace pipe is filled with the fresh catnip. Following the Cat-sop tradition, Autumn, being the newest brave, introduces herself prior to the peace pipe smoking. Autumn tells her story of being a stray cat, bringing tears to all. She then takes several puffs of the pipe and passes it to the next brave. The smoking has begun.

The fresh catnip proves to be a little too fresh and soon the community wigwam is filled with smoke. A large smoke signal of distress fills the night sky. The smoking braves become choking braves and begin a mass exodus from the wigwam.

As the braves frantically seek fresh air under the moon shine, someone tosses the lit peace pipe aside. Pipe embers scatter and catch the community wigwam on fire. The warm wigwam burns down to the sacred ground, but not before it catches a second afire. And so it goes, wigwam after wigwam, until the village's last wigwam spire falls into the pyre and the fire expires.

Having lost their entire village to the errant peace pipe, the Cat-sop Indians have gone from a surplus of mice and enough-rice-to-suffice to zero mice and zero rice. Since it's late summer, none of this can be replaced at any price. Gone, too, as a result of the fire, is their entire supply of winter clothing. The dire fire requires the braves to do what cat Indians do; they hold a pow wow, or two.

The tribal council appeals to the Great Spirit in the Sky. The sky spirit offers the following solution. He will extend the warm weather from mid-September until mid-November. This will allow enough time for the braves to replace their toasted mice and their charred rice. Delaying the start of the cold weather also gives the braves time to replace their incinerated winter attire.

Now you know the origin of the term Indian Summer. If you repeat this story to others, they will either think you're joking, or they'll check to see what you're smoking in that peace pipe you're toking.

NICKY

Darkness enters. It draws its gauze over daytime eyes, dulling visual perceptions. Yet blackness awakens other sensations. Finding myself helpless to resist the words, I write my ode to Nicky without the benefit of sight.

Slowly, gently, I caress and feel her splendor. Knowing her lovely softness and manner tender. Carefully and precisely, I paint for you an image drawn in and from the dark, as silky sweetness is drawn from cocoa hearts.

This seems the only way to write about Nicky, for she embodies the unknown. Her mystery does not fan fears but excites delight. Nicky, with a nature sweet and accepting, now waits quietly to learn who, not if any, will take her. For she knows instinctively that she will not be forsaken.

Darkness awakens and stirs imagination. Thus, I write of young Nicky in the only way I might; I tap on keys at the stroke of midnight. Nicky casts powerful magic, but being unseen, it only seems right that it's robed in the color of the night.

ELYSIAN

I'll be up front with you. I often imagine the shelter having a small room tucked away under a staircase that only a few people know about. There's a lock on the door, and only I have the key. And rightly so, since the sign on the door reads: Ed's Private Reserve. Inside you'll not find whiskey, but cats – cats I find especially intoxicating.

Once in awhile a cat comes in that I simply want to keep for myself. Can't take them all home, but they can enter my private reserve. Not locked in a back room, for this room is only a figment of my imagination, but locked away in my mind.

Elysian is such a cat. His name means characteristic of heaven or paradise. Perhaps I should stop there, for that says it all. Elysian exudes adorability. Approach him and he turns over on his back, tilts back his head, and looks at you with gorgeous green eyes. Pet him and he head-butts your hand while squirming this way and that. While his persona radiates beams of friendship, his appearance delights your sense of sight.

Elysian is a big boy, about the size of a small tiger cub, sporting dark brown tabby stripes on a golden brown coat. Accentuate that with snow white slippers and lily white cravat and you've achieved the wow level. Make no mistake, here's a dandy one from Ed's Private Reserve.

BELLE

The moon played a game of hide and seek in the partially overcast night sky. As Belle ambled along, searching, she could have been mistaken for a mere shadow. Suddenly the night breeze picked up and swept through her medium long, silver gray coat. She then seemed to shape-shift under the intermittent moonlight.

Her glistening golden eyes confirmed this was no mere shadow, but a glorious living creature. For all her glory, Belle was a rather frail creature; she repeatedly stumbled and fell. Yet, she always picked herself up and continued ambling along her search. She was searching for her home, but she was never to find it again.

Belle came to the shelter as a stray and was quite vocal, as if to say, "Dear kind ladies and sirs, this is not the home for which I have been searching!"

Her talkativeness earned her the name Decibelle. As she settled into life at the shelter, she became much less vocal and her name was shortened to simply Belle.

Ask anyone at the shelter about Belle and you will get the same response. "She's laid back and a total sweetheart."

I spent time with Belle one afternoon. It was her sparkling, golden eyes which initially attracted me to her. That flowing silvery gray coat makes her look like a real puffball. But, pet

Belle, and you discover how bony and underweight she is. She'll gain weight at the shelter, but what she needs, beyond calories and more than weight, is an abundance of love.

Belle is approximately ten years old. She exhibits that calm and accepting nature so often found in mature cats. I also observed an unmistakable spirit and zest for life in Belle.

Frankly, I found it difficult not to take Belle home with me. You might say she swung on my heart strings and tied them in knots. Oh, I know she's safe and well-cared-for at the shelter, but I also know Belle is still searching; searching for someone like you and a special place to call home, one final time.

CHESTER

Chester, dear Chester, with all that chatter, is something the matter? To call this guy a chatterbox seems rather like saying, he simply talks. Talk with this guy is so accentuated and in such rapid fire that it makes you perspire. Perhaps likening his chatter to a ticker tape or a telegraph better describes his constant patter.

When listening to Chester, you want to ask him if he's confessing. Chester, are those pent-up feelings that you're expressing? Surely it isn't simply a personal complaint that has you talking so intently without restraint.

Don't say I didn't warn you. Adopt Chester only if his unending chatter doesn't matter. Or perhaps you want a pet for company. Someone to talk to. Well, Chester definitely will talk to you. You might not get a word in edgewise, but Chester certainly will talk. To be fair, though, I'm not sure Chester will be this vocal once he's in a home. He may never be a wallflower; but at home, he may forego his imitation of Comcast and his unending broadcast.

This is a darling young male with the silkiest of tails. His entire coat is the silkiest. On a scale of one to ten, it's a ten. It's more or less a medium length. A dove gray with a white underpinning making him a handsome guy.

Chester is not shy. No, sir, Chester is not shy! He loves being held, cuddled and petted. Friendly he is without further question. And I do have one suggestion. If you want to know more about Chester, just ask him, and he'll tell you all you want to know, and more, and more.

With Chester, you will be unique among your friends. Adopt yourself a talking cat. See who can top that! It would have to be a singing dog or a dancing frog. Something like that, to outdo you and your conversationalist cat!

JASPER

Likely, you've heard the old joke: What's black and white and red all over? The answer is the newspaper, of course. Yes, I know, it's not at all funny. Admittedly, it's pretty weak.

But I have a better answer to the question, and it's certainly no joke or anything lame. I'm referring to Jasper. You'll never be ashamed of this handsome, young male tuxedo kitty. Obviously, he's black and white. But what about red?

I read Jasper the moment I laid eyes on him. Walk by his cage and he reaches out to touch you. Open his cage and he practically flings himself into your arms. Pet Jasper and he enthusiastically head-butts your hand.

I read Jasper right from the start as fiercely friendly, enormously engaging, and utterly endearing. Enclose all of that in a coat as soft as velvet and as smooth as silk and you have one dashing specimen of a cat.

Have time to kill while waiting for Jasper's adoption application to be processed so you can whiz him home? Try this. Grab a newspaper and circle all the complimentary adjectives you can find. Now read back the words you've circled. In black and white you've read all the superlatives that describe your Jasper.

"That's pretty weak, too, Ed," says the reader.

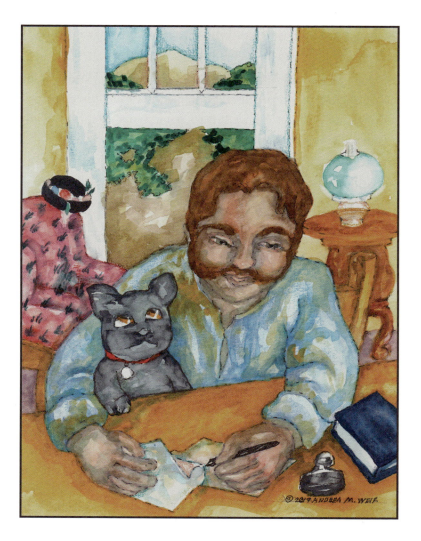

MYSTERY

No need to cross the pond to visit 221B Baker Street. The mystery can be solved without the aid of Holmes or Watson. Your search for a loving and affectionate cat has ended. No more nights without a cuddly, snuggle-bug. Our cat, Mystery, is your answer. He's a handsome cat just beyond his third year. Mystery's real beauty, though, is more than the surface. It lies in his manner. Pet him and he exudes satisfaction. He licks your hand incessantly, purrs most melodically, head-butts and squirms with pleasure. Mystery shows appreciation so fervently, you feel as though you're St. Peter at the Gate allowing him a glimpse of Heaven.

Adopt this guy and smiling will become your habit; not a coy sort of smile, but a broad smile of satisfaction. Friends and family will suspect someone has stolen your heart. And when they ask whodunit, let them puzzle over it awhile. Tell them, with a wink and a smile, it's a Mystery with you, too.

BUFFY

To understand Buffy's story, you must believe in angels. Buffy himself is an angel. You'll get no dispute there. Ask anyone who knows him. He is with us today due to a guardian angel rescuing him.

Buffy was found wandering, alone and helpless. He undeniably summons forth the better angels of our nature. Witness the outpouring of love from shelter staff, volunteers and visitors. And there is one more person, yet unknown, who will reveal the better angel of their nature when they adopt Buffy.

This is an elderly cat, maybe sixteen years old. Many would consider him pathetic looking. He was recently shaved because his long, buff coat was badly matted. He's nothing but skin and bones, and continually hobbles about. He has a strong constitution, without a doubt. Yet, this frail, innocent creature is one of the most endearing and affectionate cats I've ever encountered, with a heart of pure gold and a soul that sparkles more brilliantly than a crown full of diamonds.

How long Buffy has left on this Earth, only God knows. Those of us who love him dearly pray his remaining time will be in a loving, doting home; a home where he is showered with the affection he so fervently craves and richly deserves.

Angels. Buffy's story is all about angels. Please, God, Buffy needs one more angel to care for him here on Earth. One day you'll have Buffy in Heaven with you, God. He'll likely put a big smile on your face, too!

 ## FLO

Her ash and white coat is crafted by angels entwining dove feathers with gossamer thread. They fashion it medium in length and silky. "Quite exquisite," says an angel.

Flo's chartreuse eyes are gifted by cherubs. They capture the glow of a million fireflies. "How splendid they look on Flo!" exclaims Cupid.

Flo's gentleness and understanding stem from a golden heart. "I unlocked the pot at the end of my rainbow, giving Flo her compassionate nature," explains the proud and pleased Creator.

Are you Flo's special someone? You must be governed by romance and think in poetry, not prose. If so, I envy you. A bit of heaven shall grace your life.

CHARLESTON

He had a house full of cats. Twenty-six to be exact, all named Sam, except for one named Hester. I'm speaking of the American Icon, pop artist Andy Warhol. Warhol loved cats, and he painted cats. More correctly, he illustrated them. He illustrated them in vivid, shocking colors. Warhol's art elevated the ordinary to the glamorous and he employed a style that is not for everyone.

Which brings us to our young adult cat, Charleston. I suggest to you that he's your vintage Andy Warhol cat. Charleston elevates the common American Domestic Shorthair cat to something much more glamorous. Even his name suggests a certain sophistication. His coat, while not shocking pink, magenta or sage, is a stunning silver gray. And Charleston's tabby stripes are vivid and precise. They could have been applied to him by an illustrator.

Charleston's personality renders him a cat who is not for everyone. In addition to being timid, his previous owner said Charleston can be rather testy at times. He needs a family with no small children, and a quiet home would suit him best.

Charleston is exceedingly handsome. You might say he's quite special and he knows it. Think of him as a temperamental artist. He may not fit in just anywhere, but he's a cut above the ordinary. If you own Charleston, you'll have a devoted, loving companion. But you will also be in possession of a fine feline specimen of living, breathing art.

CORNELIA

WANTED

A kindred spirit, someone who will love, cherish,
and provide a loving home for Cornelia.

The best match would be a person who can identify with her. Someone who sees much of himself or herself in this cat. What would that person be like? And what kind of cat is Cornelia?

Ever feel you've come up short in life? Been stumbling along, tripping over one disappointment after another? And as a result, oftentimes unsure if you can maintain your balance day after day? Are you constantly chasing your dreams, but failing to realize a single one? If so, Cornelia may be the cat for you!

Cornelia has likely traveled countless miles and many a winding road over her ten years. Chances are at least a few of those roads were ones less taken; bumpy trails with exasperating trials. No doubt these have contributed to Cornelia being the cat she is today.

Frankly, she's not very effusive; not all sweetness, cuddles and purrs, unlike some cats. Yet, Cornelia has her moments of being affectionate. She certainly loves to lap sit, but you must handle her as SHE deems appropriate. Be sensitive, show her deference, and relate to her in an understanding way. Cornelia has an abundance of love to give. But you must learn how to tap into it. One must act astutely to help Cornelia reach her potential.

Sounds familiar? You say that could be a description of yourself? Just as I suspected. So, there IS someone out there for Cornelia! I'd love to see her matched with such a kindred soul – someone like you.

Cornelia is quite a petite lady. She has a smoky gray coat with touches of a lighter gray (I call it frosting) on her mask, leggings and mittens. She's a tabby cat with only the slightest hint of stripes. They're most prominent on her legs – sturdy legs that have carried her over those many miles.

She recently took a road less taken, losing an eye; not from an accident but for medical reasons. But today Cornelia is healthy and years lie ahead of her.

If you can identify with Cornelia, she's eminently qualified to be your pet. And perhaps she'll be something a bit more; sort of a co-pilot helping you traverse troubled waters. She's likely done so herself. Two can navigate better than one. Two hearts can better endure hardship and, yes, ensure there will be occasional fun. Two souls can better transform a troubled life. Cornelia needs someone. And I believe it's best she finds someone who also needs her.

Adopt this girl. Together, turn your stumbles into dance. Turn your disappointments into triumphs. Own your dreams, making them daily realities. Unlock Cornelia and she'll be steady, reliable, and a loving companion. She's experienced and has been tested. Unquestionably, she's the real deal.

THE FAMILY CHRISTMAS TREE

My mother never knew her father. He died when she was very young. A faint visual image and the vague sense that he was present in her earliest childhood memories was all she ever had. She was four when he passed, leaving behind a cat named Chalmers who soon bonded with my mother. The two of them became inseparable best buddies.

My mother would recount how they ran through the house playing, often some version of hide and seek. She always confided in that cat, too. He was a loving, steady influence and she claimed he made her feel secure. I remember her saying that Chalmers helped fill the void of not having a father in her life. She felt she could always count on Chalmers. Always. Except for a certain Christmas Eve.

The annual Christmas tree was a huge event in my mother's life. Months before Christmas, she and her mother began making paper and clay ornaments to hang on the tree, along with the antique glass bulbs that had been in the family for generations.

Mother often daydreamed of the December day when her two brothers would cut down a tree in the grove of young pines back of the barn, and then place the tree in the front parlor for the entire family to decorate.

One year, as the tree stood there in its glittering splendor, my mother ran through the room with Chalmers in close pursuit. Chalmers failed to negotiate a hairpin turn and leapt for safety, landing in the Christmas tree. He was a big cat, and the tree came crashing down. Broken family heirlooms and broken Christmas dreams were interspersed with broken pine branches on the parlor floor. The tree could not be salvaged, and my mother cried and blamed Chalmers. But that lasted merely through Christmas Day.

Chalmers died ten years later on another Christmas Eve. He was buried in the grove of pine trees back of the barn. Each Christmas thereafter, Mother said she thought of Chalmers on Christmas Eve. Not how he crashed the tree, but that he was buried in the small grove of pine trees back of the barn.

It took someone as astute and intuitive as my mother to point out that by being returned to the earth in that grove of trees, Chalmers helped provide the family with a beautiful new Christmas tree year after year. She viewed that as Chalmers' way of repaying the family (but I knew she meant herself) for that long ago destroyed Christmas dream.

MING

When I look at Ming I'm reminded of the Chinese porcelain of the same name. Like this fine ceramic pottery, our cat Ming has

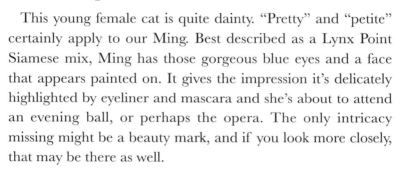

elaborate design and vivid colors.

This young female cat is quite dainty. "Pretty" and "petite" certainly apply to our Ming. Best described as a Lynx Point Siamese mix, Ming has those gorgeous blue eyes and a face that appears painted on. It gives the impression it's delicately highlighted by eyeliner and mascara and she's about to attend an evening ball, or perhaps the opera. The only intricacy missing might be a beauty mark, and if you look more closely, that may be there as well.

And of course Ming has the characteristic 'M' on her forehead. In this instance most definitely standing for Ming. This girl is such a beauty, it is my duty to sing her praises!

Her coat is most stunning with two colors of cream and tan. Did I say yet that I'm Ming's biggest fan? Personality wise, Ming is so new to us, it's hard to say. If I had to, I'd say she's still quite timid and shy. I believe, though, that by and by, our Ming would likely step up to the call and show herself to be the belle of the ball.

KITTY BOO CHERRY

He's a real corker. Like, let's pop the cork on a bottle of champagne. It's time to celebrate! It seems every year we have a standout kitten who simply knocks your socks off. Last year we had Flea, this year it's Kitty Boo Cherry.

Such kittens are worth celebrating by virtue of their unforgettable personality. We can never be sure of their nature when mature, but as kittens, they have everyone talking.

I think of Kitty Boo Cherry as a refreshing cherry cola, sweet and bubbly; a cherry cola with a generous shot of bourbon added! The little guy's got kick and he's very intoxicating.

If your life is in a rut, this kitten could well be the kick-start you need. He's more fun than a barrel of monkeys for those of you who have the energy to swing through your daily jungle like Tarzan or Jane.

Kitty Boo Cherry is a real looker, too. Seldom will you see a more gorgeous coat than the one worn by this silver gray tabby. Big, I mean unbelievably big and bold, black stripes highlight this guy. Think zebra and you're not far afield.

All you lovers of monkeys, zebras, Tarzan and Jane, take notice. We have a most singular kitten to celebrate and get adopted.

Seldom do I write about kittens, but I couldn't resist a word or two about this one. Come get a taste of Kitty Boo Cherry. He might uncork a sweeter and more bubbly little 'ole you!

EMMA

We join Emma in a previous lifetime. *This must be clearly understood, or nothing wonderful can come of the story I am about to share. (Dickens)*

Her beauty and dignified manner serve her well, as Emma is royalty. She's the Queen of Sheba. A caravan of camels accompany Emma on her long journey to visit the king. Riding on the camels are our cat volunteers, doing surprisingly well, since none have ridden a camel before.

Emma is being carried on a litter. I speak of a sedan chair, not of a group of kittens or latrine sand that clumps. Her lovely head and amazing green eyes sway to a certain rhythm. Two young male cats, on hind legs and wearing loincloths, step in unison carrying her litter. The caravan slowly moves along under the hot desert sun.

Emma is a mature cat of some thirteen years and is known for her keen intelligence. She seems to possess an innate understanding of human behavior and is about to perform a symbolic act. While the litter sways and the caravan rumbles, Emma tosses lifesaver candies to the volunteers. The candy is caught in mid air as the volunteers bounce up and down wildly on their camels.

It's a heartwarming scene, and life never tasted sweeter to the cat volunteers, many of whom experience a sugar high, causing them to bounce uncontrollably. Having become unbalanced, several riders slide down the hump of their camels and land on the desert floor. They struggle, but eventually manage to lift themselves off the scorching sand, returning to their camels as half-baked volunteers. (no comment)

Once the caravan arrives at the palace, Emma presents gifts to the king. Her gift of spices, she explains, represents her manner. She can be sweet, but also a bit tart, though never sour. At her age, though, she's mellowed to mostly honey. Her gift of gold, she says, represents her Bengal coat, ranging from a luscious brown and orange to glistening golden. Lastly, her gift of jewels resembles her emerald eyes, as gleaming and bright as any gem in her kingdom.

Emma has possessed these very traits from one lifetime to another. Assuredly, you'll take home the Queen of Sheba, if you're wise enough to adopt the most majestic Emma.

HARLEY

Harley has put on a bit of mileage over his thirteen years. Covering those miles, he's learned a thing or two about handling himself. So there's some wear and tear. Yet, Harley's become the consummate sweetheart and is most entertaining to be around. He's a generator of smiles.

At the shelter, Harley is frequently used to test whether a dog will accept a cat. Not a problem for Harley. Likely, he's met many a K-9 putting on those miles. Harley once accidentally bumped into another cat as they explored the adoption room. With many cats this would have led to a spat, but not with Harley. The two cats simply touched noses several times and passed on by. As I said, Harley's a generator of smiles.

Harley wears a gorgeous coat, a long-haired tabby with an array of colors. Earth tones perhaps representing all the places he has visited during his travels.

Harley's no spring chicken, but then maybe you're no baby chick yourself. In which case, here's a delightfully affectionate and friendly traveling companion. And when the two of you come to the end of the road, perhaps you'll fly the coop together. As I said, Harley's no spring chicken, but he's sure a generator of smiles.

WILLIAM

When a cat reminds one of Shakespeare, methinks he merits a bit of prose. So with pen in hand, I propose to compose my impressions of William.

It started rather innocently. I paid a visit to the shelter and Linda said she wanted me to meet an exceptionally sweet cat named William. As I headed to the cat room, my mind was churning. It kept repeating, "William, Sweet William."

"Oh yes," I thought. "Sweet William is a flower." In fact, I recall reading it had been the favorite flower of a very famous William. Shakespeare was said to have found the color and fragrance of the Sweet William seductive as he frequently strolled along the banks of the River Avon.

What does this have to do with our cat William? For starters, William, indeed, is one sweet cat! Referring to him as Sweet William seems a natural thing to do. When we met, he greeted my outstretched hand with a gentle head-butt, as if to say, "Pleased to make your acquaintance." He's certainly personable and affectionate, too. The manner in which he rubs up against you while constantly purring is endearing beyond belief.

Colorful? The Sweet William flower has nothing over our cat when it comes to dazzling one's sense of sight. William's golden brown tabby stripes seem to glow and provide a dramatic contrast to their ebony companions. William is eye candy with an added measure of zip and pizzazz.

Gentlemanly? For a three-year-old stray cat, William has a remarkably laid back, genteel and mature quality about him. He seems comfortable in his own skin, as if he's a learned and wise being, a Shakespearean kind of thing.

As I say, it started rather innocently. But thanks to dear Linda, it's ended with great fanfare. Think fireworks in a 4th of July sky, for that's what William does for me. Oh yes, I'm mightily impressed with this wonderfully uncommon cat. And I venture to bet he'll impress the Dickens out of each and every one of you!

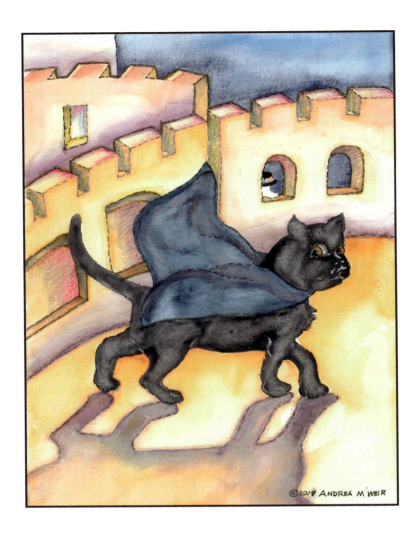

DRACULA

He's lithe and lean. His athleticism stuns you as he prowls about. You notice his long strides and how he keeps low to the ground. The Count reminds me of a panther.

Envision him roaming the cold and damp corridors of a castle. He's the castle's lifeblood circulating through its veins. In dimly lit halls, he barely can be seen. For he's the color of the night. His eyes reveal his location, though, as they flash golden and bright. The glow of his eyes rivals the blazing torches affixed to the castle walls.

If there is such a thing as a sexy cat, The Count is it. He's as sexy and seductive as his namesake. His purrs are hypnotic and his playfulness lures you in. You're a helpless victim to his allure.

Be careful, though, he'll bite! Not literally. But he'll sap your affection and you'll turn into putty as you cuddle him. But this relationship is not one-sided. You will enliven and energize each other.

This black-cloaked fellow from Transylvania will transform your home into a castle. He's exotic enough and intriguing enough to do just that. Count on it!

MOSES

"I can't believe you're doing this, Ed!"

"Oh Moses, cool it! No one will even miss you."

"I'm Pet of the Week. How can you say no one will miss me? With all that media coverage, it's likely potential adopters will seek me out. You, yourself, wrote that I'm a spectacularly splendid cat. But rather than me getting adopted this week, you put me in a cardboard box, about to shove me under your seat."

"Hush, Moses, we're about to take off. But first I need to tuck that beautiful, flourishing tail of yours back into the box with the rest of you. As I've told you before, your ravishing, long black coat and swashbuckling tail remind me of Zorro, cape, sword and all!"

"Excuse me, sir. I've been overhearing your conversation with that cardboard box. Are you feeling a bit light-headed? Should I call a flight attendant?"

"No need for that. I have a very personable cat in that box."

"You were having a conversation with a cat? Cats don't talk, sir. I'm calling the flight attendant!"

"Yes, ma'am, it's a cat. His name is Moses. He's three years old and has a charming and engaging manner. You might say he has an 'arresting' personality, but that could be misconstrued and alarm other passengers.

"Moses is quite friendly; also soft and cuddly, kind of like these flotation devices were sitting on. Look out the window, ma'am. That pitch black sky streaked with starlight resembles Moses' long, flowing coat. And the moon over there, with it's soft golden glow, is the color of Moses' eyes.

"Yes, Moses is a striking cat. He nearly takes your breath away. Lucky those oxygen masks are up there, just in case!"

"Moses, wake up!"

"Oh, hi Sonja."

"Sorry to wake you from your sweet dreams, Moses, but it's morning and I'm here to clean your cage."

"No problem. In fact, I'm quite grateful. That was no sweet dream I was having. More like a nightmare. I was in a plane with Ed, 35,000 feet over the Rockies, and headed to Pittsburgh. Pittsburgh, of all places!"

SISSY

This is for all the opera aficionados out there. Like maybe two or three of you? Okay, maybe one, if I'm lucky!

Allow me to introduce, Sissy, the Maria Callas of our adoption room. Sissy is a young feline just coming into her prime, say three-years-old and some change. Sissy has become the prima donna of the adoption room.

Prissy Miss Sissy. She's a temperamental princess, and on certain days may be a drama queen. Sissy has appointed herself our greeter. She's often perched high on a shelf, her improvised balcony.

But let visitors enter our stage and Sissy is often the first to meet them. And she's always noticed, too. In addition to her charming exterior, she greets them with an aria of her own composition.

Sissy is quite vocal and there is no competition to be found. She'll begin with bel canto quite like Maria, and if the sweet melody doesn't do the trick, Sissy will do a quick switch. There will be a deafening cadenza until she gets proper notice. And our visitors fall for her act. She garners more attention than any other cat.

Visitors express delight with such a vocal kitty. They pet and praise her until they are grazed by Sissy's paw. As I said, she's a temperamental princess. She dotes on affection, but on her terms. Sissy is most highly regarded when on stage and performing her best. She's often praised as a sassy young kitty, and her feistiness many simply adore.

Sissy is dressed for the stage, too. Her dazzling costume is a light brown tabby with golden highlights with a striking white bib. She's fairly small in stature, but her personality dwarfs all others currently on our stage.

If you want personality and sass, here's a kitty whose first class sass cannot be surpassed. You will never find another cat with the pizzazz, stage presence and razzmatazz of our Sissy!

LILLIE

It was an unusual feeling. Déjà vu, perhaps, for that French term literally means "seen before." I thought I had seen Lillie previously in a dream.

Maybe that was it. But then it hit me. It was as if I smacked my head while opening a door. But a door to where? The hot afternoon sun peeked through ancient firs. Shade from the trees kept the grass a luscious green, even though it was late August.

As I reached the top of a small rise, I was startled and found myself exclaiming, "Look there, a cat!" But as I pointed, the cat vanished. I was certain, though, that I had seen a cat sitting there motionless, next to a tombstone.

I was even more startled when I met Lillie at the shelter a few days later. In fact, I became convinced it was Lillie I saw in that cemetery. She looks unique enough not to be confused with another cat. It's not every day you see a dilute tortie. Certainly not one as interesting in coloring and coat pattern as Lillie. And her jade green eyes are unmistakable. Lillie entered the shelter two weeks before my trip to the cemetery.

I enjoy visiting cemeteries, particularly older ones. I find them peaceful and I'm often fascinated by the out-of-fashion names and inscriptions on the stones. That explains why I was in the cemetery. But if it actually was Lillie I saw, how could she have been there? Lillie tends to be an independent, difficult cat to know. She's laid back and has a certain maturity about her.

When considering Lillie's persona, I'm reminded of the proverb, *still waters run deep*. There's passion there, but Lillie conceals it. Get to know her, and she'll bond quickly, becoming a loyal and affectionate cat. If you own Lillie, she's likely your soulmate. Maybe cats do live nine lives. Maybe the emotional bond between Lillie and her owner in a previous life was so strong that their spirits have never parted.

Consider adopting this extraordinary cat while you occupy the same realm of reality. It's a chance of a lifetime. Take Lillie home and walk together through doors into the unknown. Keep in mind, though, your journey with Lillie literally might go on forever.

APOLLO

I met Apollo by tripping over her. It was the perfect introduction. From that point on my heart was in a free fall. The sky parted, the planets danced, and the moon and sun sung to me a silly love song. Okay, that may be a bit over the top, but I've never encountered a cat as quirky and appealing as Apollo.

She's an odd-looking thing, but adorably so. Stocky build on a small frame, with an unusually-shaped head that kind of looks like a triangle. She has beady, penetrating yellow eyes, and a dirty white coat with two exceptions. Her long tail, much too long for her body, is dark gray, and there's a large gray spot on the top of her head.

Her appearance is amusing, more so than it is attractive. But it fits her personality to a T. If Apollo had been born a human, she'd likely be the most popular comedian of her time. She's a total hoot to watch. Flies about like Looney Tunes' Roadrunner, her antics causing mischief, and always eliciting laughter from those lucky enough to see.

Apollo is personable, too. In fact, she's your ultimate puppy cat. Unlike most cats, when you call her name she immediately comes running, lands on your lap, and licks, licks, licks. Never known a cat givin' such good lickin'. Even her name puts a smile on my face.

Apollo is the god of music, poetry and art, and is depicted as a handsome, young athletic male. Our middle-aged female cat, Apollo, is the antithesis of her namesake. To me she's a goddess, but it's of silliness, laughter and fun.

MY BROTHER'S KEEPER

I own four cats, if anyone can be said to own a cat. Each was adopted from a shelter. This story focuses on the interaction among three of them. The factor dictating their behavior is the limited vision of my cat, Chance. I don't mean he lacks inspiration and creativity. He was born nearly blind.

Chance is a relatively young and exceedingly handsome Lynx Point Siamese. I find it heartwarming and uplifting how my other cats not only seem to realize Chance does not see well, but they have modified their own behavior to assist Chance in compensating for his handicap.

The primary hero is my cat Charlie. This shouldn't surprise me, since Charlie is one of the most impressive cats I've ever encountered. Visually, he's striking, being a Snowshoe/Rag doll mix. He's extremely social and well behaved.

From day one, Chance and Charlie got along amazingly well. No getting acquainted period was needed. They bonded the moment they met. The two are now inseparable, joined at the hip as it were. If Chance experiences difficulty due to his limited vision, Charlie has learned to help him out.

Chance occasionally becomes disoriented. We have a second home tucked away near the end of the world in Washington state. Going from one house to the other always confuses Chance. Charlie has learned to rub up against Chance and they walk in tandem until Chance realizes which house he's navigating. There are other examples, too, of Charlie always being there to guide Chance in the right direction.

My cat Calypso is a petite tuxie who came to the shelter as a nearly feral kitten. Calypso was at the shelter for nearly a year and had made only limited progress with socialization.

For some reason she took a liking to me. One night I dreamt I had adopted Calypso, and several days later I did just that.

She's been with us three years now and has been a total sweetheart, with one qualifier. She doesn't like the other cats and throws a hissing fit if one gets near her. Yet, she's learned not to do this with Chance. If he approaches, she seems to realize he doesn't see her. She'll scamper away when he gets too close, but seldom does she hiss at him.

Cain queried God as to whether he was his brother's keeper. Through the hand of God, my cats seem to have answered that question. I admit, I don't read the Bible. But I do read and learn from my cats. My own belief is that God smiles upon that, while breathing a sigh of relief.

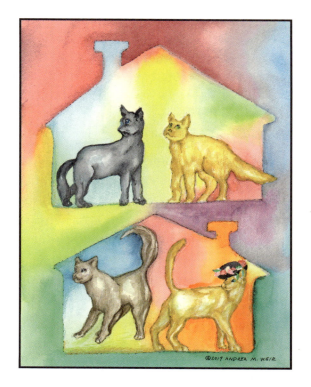

A FINAL WORD

"Ed, are you trying to say your book is finished? I've read and reread your silly draft and there's no mention of your girl, Cairo. I was the first cat you owned, long before these other cats came into our home. Yet, your book tells nothing of Cairo. I'm the cat with a heart of pure gold, at least that's what I've always been told. What about the countless times you've whispered in my ear, 'I love my little gray turtle dove?' Yet, you're not going to write about Cairo?"

Dear Cairo,

Haven't you heard the expression, saving the best for last? That's what I intended for you, sweet Cairo. But I could find no rhyme or verse, nor lengthy discourse, which adequately expresses my feelings for you. So, thank you, my cherished one, for writing about yourself. Once again, you've been there to help me out. For over ten years I've been able to rely upon you. So, as a tribute, I give you the final word in my book, and that word is Cairo!

"Oh, Ed, that's sweet. But us cats wanna choose the book's final word. We've been talking among ourselves and realize, with your book nearing completion and all, none of us will have the ability to talk much longer. So we thought we'd better speak up now, while we still can.

"You featured each of us in your book, right? And without such featuring, why, you'd have no writing, and the readers would have no reading. So us cats got to thinking. We deserve some rewarding! We propose this book ends with TREATS. We'll settle for a six month supply – each, that is.

The final word, Mr. Ed, is TREATS!"